Anonymous

**Common Observances and Explanations**

of some of the rules of the Sisters of Charity of the B.V.M., St. Joseph's Convent, Dubuque County, Iowa / compiled at the desire of Mother M.F. Clarke

Anonymous

**Common Observances and Explanations**
*of some of the rules of the Sisters of Charity of the B.V.M., St. Joseph's Convent, Dubuque County, Iowa / compiled at the desire of Mother M.F. Clarke*

ISBN/EAN: 9783337428372

Printed in Europe, USA, Canada, Australia, Japan

Cover: Foto ©Lupo / pixelio.de

More available books at **www.hansebooks.com**

# COMMON OBSERVANCES

AND

### Explanations of Some of the Rules

OF THE

# SISTERS OF CHARITY,

OF THE

### B. V. M.

## ST. JOSEPH'S CONVENT,

DUBUQUE COUNTY, IOWA.

COMPILED AT THE DESIRE OF OUR VENERATED FOUNDRESS

MOTHER M. F. CLARKE.

—

1892

# PREFACE.

1. In this book of "Common Observances, etc.," our Community will find a collection of the practices and forms most commonly employed by us in the discharge of our several duties, both spiritual and temporal, since the earliest days of its existence—many of these customs having been either adopted or introduced by our Very Rev. Founder, Father DONAGHOE, as aids to the observance of our Rules and to the promotion of uniformity among us in the fulfillment of our duties. Now that time has tested their utility, we have been taught to prize them as well calculated to effect that for which they were intended. Therefore, along with some explanations that a few of our Rules seemed to require, we have collected these Customs into a little book, for more convenient reference, that, as time progresses and our numbers increase, these worthy practices may not fall into disuse.

2. Many of us can still recall the days when, a feeble few, we began these observances under the immediate care and companionship of our beloved Founder and Father, and our gentle, tender-hearted Mother Foundress—Mary Frances Clarke—both of happy memory.

# CHAPTER I.

## ON OUR SPIRITUAL EXERCISES.

(SECOND CHAPTER OF THE RULE.)

1. On rising in the morning, each Sister makes the Sign of the Cross, as a consecration of the day to God's service, and dresses herself with all possible modesty and diligence, at the same time reciting, or responding to, in an audible voice, the customary prayer to be said while dressing, viz.: the prayer for rising, a decade of the Rosary and the De Profundis for the repose of the souls of the faithful who died during the night, and the indulgenced aspirations to Jesus, Mary and Joseph, thereby renewing the oblation of ourselves to this most Holy Family, which, by our Constitutions, we are to take for our model in all our actions.

2. Having concluded these vocal prayers, let each one recall to mind the points read on the evening previous for the morning's meditation. Twenty minutes are allowed for the toilet; at the expiration of which the bell rings for morning prayers, five minutes being allowed for the Sisters

to assemble in the chapel or oratory. The Sister appointed for the duty of reciting the prayers shall do so in a clear, audible voice. She shall recite the vocal prayers prescribed by the Rules. On Sunday and Friday, the Litany of the Holy name of Jesus; on Monday and Wednesday, the Litany of St. Joseph; on Thursday, the Litany of the Blessed Sacrament; on Tuesday and Saturday, the Litany of the Blessed Virgin. After the vocal prayers, all stand and make an act of the presence of God, the Lector saying aloud, " Let us place ourselves in the presence of God." Then, all kneeling, she recites aloud the preparatory prayer for meditation, which is followed by the first point of the meditation—ten minutes for each point—one-half hour for the whole meditation. To prevent distraction from fatigue or drowsiness, our Rev. Founder recommended change of posture, therefore we kneel during the reading of the points, and sit during meditation. However, each Sister is free to assume the position which will best aid her in making meditation well. We must be careful to make the act of the Presence of God with great faith and fervor, as the sense of the Presence of God is our best protection against the natural slothfulness and tepidity that might hinder us from meditating profitably; besides, the soul impressed with the Divine Presence becomes more sensible of her own deficiency and weakness, and so is impelled to fly to God for strength and grace.

3. At the conclusion of the meditation, we recite the prayer of St. Ignatius, "Soul of Christ," review, for five minutes, the manner in which we have made our meditation, then recite the prayer, "O Holy Virgin," etc., and end by the offering of the duties of the day, in union with those of our Lord Jesus Christ whilst upon earth, and the prayer, "May the most Divine Heart," etc.

4. The "Angelus" is to be *said when the bell rings*. Should this interrupt another spiritual exercise, it should be only while we say the *Angelus proper*, ending with the prayer, "Pour forth we beseech Thee O Lord," etc. Where no "An gelus bell" rings, we say the Angelus with the community prayers.

5. The hour for Mass, at the Mother House, is generally six A. M. On the missions it may not be convenient for the Rev. Pastor to celebrate at a fixed hour, and in such a case, it may be necessary for the Sisters to breakfast and even perform some of their household duties before Mass. The Sister Superior will so arrange that the duties are performed with order, and that no Sister be obliged to remain from Mass, when a proper management of her time and duty would prevent

such a spiritual loss. They should all leave the house and return together in proper order. It is customary for all to kneel during low Mass, except the sick and the aged.

6. During the day, when the clock strikes, we recite the customary prayer in honor of the Sacred Heart of Jesus, an Ave Maria to ask the protection of the Blessed Virgin at the hour of our death, and the prayer "Eternal Rest," etc., for all the souls of the Faithful departed. In presence of strangers, instead of this prayer may be said mentally, "Blessed be the hour in which our Lord Jesus Christ was born and suffered for us." It is our custom that the Superior, and, in her absence, the Sister longest professed, recite this prayer, as well as "Grace" before and after meals.

7. The daily Prayers and Office on Sundays are recited, and spiritual lectures read, by the Lector appointed for the week.

8. At the Mother House, the bell rings for the Particular Examen, at a quarter before twelve. On the missions, the Sisters must repair to the chapel or oratory to make their Examen, as soon as the pupils are dismissed.

9. The Superior shall name the book to be read during dinner, and she will be careful to see that a chapter from the ."Imitation" be read first.

Immediately after dinner we make a visit to the Blessed Sacrament, reciting the prayers named in the list for this occasion. Where we cannot visit the Blessed Sacrament, we are to say these prayers, either in the oratory or refectory, as the Superior shall direct.

10. At the Mother House a general visit to the Blessed Sacrament is made at two o'clock P. M. On the missions this visit is to be made also, but as it cannot be at the same hour, unless in vacation, the Superior of each house must appoint the time best suited to the convenience of the Sisters. The prayers, both at home and in the mission, will be the same.

11. Half an hour's spiritual reading is to precede night prayers. Having recited the invocation to the Holy Ghost, a Sister will read, in a voice loud enough to be heard by all present, a book approved for the purpose, generally St. Liguori's "Nun Sanctified," or Rodriguez's "Christian Perfection," or some such book treating on religious subjects.

12. After the spiritual reading, the night prayers prescribed in the list of Community Prayers are said. Then follows *the General Examen*, according to the formula.

13. On the last Sunday of the month, instead of the Office of the Blessed Virgin, we recite the

Office of the Dead for our deceased members. As the Rule ordains that we shall say the little Office of the Blessed Virgin on Sundays and festivals of obligation, should a Sister be *necessarily* prevented from reciting it with the Community, she must say the six Paters and Aves in thanksgiving to the Blessed Trinity for the Immaculate Conception.

14. On the anniversary of each Sister's death, a Pater and Ave will be said at all the Community prayers, for the happy repose of her soul.

15. When several Sisters are engaged together during the hours of silence, they may recite, in a moderate tone, vocal prayers, as the "Beads for the Dead," the Rosary of the Sacred Heart, etc., but they are not to do so when the work is noisy or requires frequent interruptions, such as laundry work, etc. When so engaged, they will do well to occupy themselves with reflections on the morning's meditation, the Presence of God, the shortness of life, the obligations of their calling, etc., not in a way, though, to weary or sadden the mind, but with a holy joy, making frequent use of ejaculatory prayers, which are so pleasing to God and so richly endowed with Indulgences by our Holy Mother, the Church.

16. At the Mother House, two or three hours are daily given to the Adoration of the Blessed

Sacrament; when it can be done, at least one hour daily should be given on the Mission, two Sisters going one-half hour each day, according to "number," until all have taken their turns.

This custom of Adoration was introduced by our Rev. Founder, as a reparation for some horrible sacrileges committed in this country, therefore we will still offer our poor prayers in the same spirit, to atone, as far as our merciful Savior will deign to accept, for the insults He is hourly receiving in the Most Holy Sacrament of the Altar, and to implore His grace and special blessing to save us from such a misfortune as to wound His loving Heart by even the least infidelity.

17. When the Sisters meet one another in passing through the house, and also on entering a room where any member of the Community may be, they will say the little aspiration, ordained by our Rev. Founder, "Praise be to Jesus, Mary and Joseph!" to which the others will respond, "Now and forevermore, Amen."

18. Every year there will be a general Retreat held at the Mother House and at the largest central missions, to which all the Sisters at the neighboring houses will repair for their Retreat and the Renovation of Vows.

The Novices on trial, if approved of according

to the conditions of the Rule, will make this Retreat at the Mother House, and be admitted to the religious profession.

### OF CONFESSION.

1. At the Mother House, the Sisters go to Confession on Thursday—the professed first, and, as much as possible, according to "number" or the order of their profession. On the missions the Superior will ask the Confessor to appoint the hour most convenient for him to hear the Sisters' Confessions.

2. Should it happen on any mission, that the Confessor be prevented, by his sacred duties, from hearing the Sisters' Confessions at the usual time, they should not complain, but cheerfully submit to the unavoidable privation, and prepare all the more fervently for the Holy Sacraments, when the opportunity presents.

3. In approaching the tribunal of Penance, we must endeavor to prepare ourselves with such diligence as not to occupy any more of the Confessor's time than is needed; for this reason we recite the "Confiteor" before entering the Confessional. We should, if possible, perform our Sacramental penance before leaving the church.

4. The Sister Superior will request the Rev. Pastor to apply to the Bishop of the Diocese for the appointment of an Extraordinary Confessor

for the Sisters, at the quarter-tenses, as named in our Rules.

### HOLY COMMUNION.

1. Our Sisters will be careful to approach the Holy Table with the utmost reverence and devotion, which should be discernible in their manner, neatness of attire, and their whole exterior.

2. As the general Holy Communions are offered for some specified intention, according to the Rule, each Sister should be careful to offer her Holy Communion for that intention, and to say the prayers prescribed, as the submission to obedience enhances the value of these devotions so richly Indulgenced by the Church.

3. The Sisters will approach Holy Communion, if possible, in the order of their profession, with hands joined before the breast, and return to their places in the same order. Let them be on their guard in making their Thanksgiving, to avoid taking any notice of the other communicants or the administration of the Sacrament.

4. The twenty-five minutes to be spent in Thanksgiving are to be counted from the time of receiving Holy Communion, not from the end of Mass.

5. We should be very particular to assist at the ceremonies of the church in a uniform manner; for instance, all should stand and kneel or sit

at the same time. To do this, we should understand beforehand what services are to take place, and so prepare for them that all may understand the ceremonies, especially of Holy Week.

6. When assisting at the Holy Sacrifice of the Mass, or other Offices of the Church, we must carefully avoid all unnecessary motions or gestures of body, also repeated coughing, rattling of beads, and all such things by which annoyance or cause of distraction might be given to others; we must also preserve a grave and collected appearance, and guard against recognizing friends and acquaintances, on entering or leaving the church; but pass in and out in a way to attract as little attention as possible.

# CHAPTER II.

### FORMULA OF GENERAL EXAMEN.

Let us place ourselves in the Presence of God.

Let us return thanks for graces received, *Creation, Redemption, Vocation to Religion, Particular Graces.*

Let us ask for light to know our defects. Recite, "Come, Holy Ghost," etc.

Let us examine ourselves on the following points: At night, before falling to sleep, did I call to mind the subject of the Meditation?

On awaking, did I fix my thoughts on the Meditation, excluding all other subjects?

When distracted, did I endeavor to recall the subject of the Meditation?

Did I make use of short aspirations or colloquies in the course of the Meditation, even if they did not come naturally?

MASS.—Did I make a formal intention for which I offered the Holy Sacrifice?

Did I make a Spiritual Communion and offer myself to our Dear Lord?

ON COMMUNION DAYS.— Did I prepare by greater recollection from the evening before?

VISIT TO THE BLESSED SACRAMENT.—Was I faithful in making the prescribed visit?

DUTIES.— Have I performed my appointed duties in union with the Holy Family at Nazareth—with care and neatness—with fervor and devotion?

Have I a pure and upright intention in all my thoughts and actions?

Have I faithfully corresponded to Divine inspirations?

OBEDIENCE.—Have I been perfectly submissive to my Superiors? Did I obey the bells promptly? Have I made known reasons of absence from common exercises to my Superior, as soon as possible, without murmuring interiorly or exteriorly?

POVERTY.—Have I been wasteful in charges? Content with what was allowed? Have I received or given anything without permission?

CHARITY.—Have I been charitable in conversation—obliging in manner—polite—not interrupting others?

If I have given offense, have I asked pardon?

Have I borne patiently the defects and peculiarities of others?

## COMMON OBSERVANCES.

Have I given advice or example contrary to the perfection of my vocation?

Have I, in anything, acted through human respect?

Have I sought my own ease—failed to assist my Sisters when I could have done so? Have I meddled in matters that did not concern me?

SILENCE.—Have I kept silence—*rejecting idle thoughts—avoiding useless words—unnecessary noise?*

MEALS.—Have I been attentive during "Grace" —taken my meals with moderation, modesty and purity of intention? Have I been attentive to those near me? Have I eaten out of the appointed time and place without permission?

RECREATION.—Have I been exact as to *time* and *place* of taking recreation? Have I mortified repugnances and inclinations, by associating with different Sisters? Did I avoid *idleness— worldly conversations — rudeness in language, tone and manner?*

MODESTY.—Do I observe religious modesty in all my words and actions?

Did I observe modesty of the eyes, especially in meeting others?

RETIRING TO REST.—Have I observed "*Sol-*

*emn Silence"*—retired to rest at the appointed time?

Let us humble ourselves for the faults we have committed.

Ask God's pardon, relying on His goodness and mercy.

Let us promise to do better next time, avoiding the faults into which we have fallen.

Ask God's grace to keep this our promise.

Return thanks to God for whatever good thoughts He has inspired us with.

### ACT OF CONTRITION.

N. B. This Formula is to be read aloud at the *Evening Examen* only.

The prayers before and after Particular Examen are to be said aloud according to the Formula of General Examen, and should occupy about four minutes; the remaining six minutes are to be spent in private examen.

### COMMUNITY PRAYERS.

#### MORNING.

Pater, Ave, Creed, Confiteor. Acts of Faith, Hope, Charity and Contrition, three Aves for the local Pastor, Litany, one-half hour's Meditation, "O Holy Virgin, etc.," "O My God! to Thee, etc.," "May the Most Divine Heart of Jesus, etc."

## COMMON OBSERVANCES. 19

###### AFTER DINNER.

Pater, Ave, Creed, Aspiration to the Sacred Heart, three Aves imploring God's blessing on the fruits of the earth from March 24 to November 1,—from November 1 to March 25, in thanksgiving for all His favors and graces,—"O Holy Angel of God, etc.," Prayer for the Pope,—"May the Most Divine Heart, etc."

###### VISIT TO THE BLESSED SACRAMENT.

Twelve Aves for Rev. Father Donaghoe; Five decades of the Rosary for the Souls in Purgatory —intention for the Community; Pater and Ave for the Bishop of Dubuque; Salve Regina for the Monks of Melleray; "May the Most Divine Heart, etc."

###### AFTER SUPPER.

Three Paters and Aves in honor of the Blessed Trinity; Pater and Ave for Rev. Father Donaghoe and deceased members; Pater and Ave for our benefactors; Salve Regina for Mother; "May the Most Divine Heart, etc."

###### NIGHT PRAYERS.

Pater, Ave, Creed, Confiteor, Pater and Ave in honor of St. Claud; Act of Consecration to St. Joseph; Seven Dolors of the Blessed Virgin; ten minutes' examen of conscience, Act of Contrition, Points of Meditation for next morning, read; "O

Holy Virgin, etc.," "O My God! to Thee, etc.," "May the Most Divine Heart, etc."

CATALOGUE OF TIME.

1. At the Mother House, the time for rising shall continue as heretofore, in Summer at 4:30, in Winter, 5 A. M. By dispensation of Mother-General, the hour of rising, in the Missions, may be 5 A. M. at all times.

2. After twenty minutes for dressing and toilet, the signal is given for morning prayer and meditation, five minutes being allowed for assembling, before morning prayer or any other exercise begins.

3. Daily Mass, Breakfast and Spiritual Lecture vary with the hour for rising, at the Mother House; Mass, in Summer, at 6, in Winter, at 6:30 A. M.—Particular Examen, 11:45,—Dinner, 12.

4. Particular Examen on Missions and Dinner, the same if possible.

5. Time allowed for Breakfast and Supper, 20 minutes,—for Dinner, 30 minutes.

6. Schools open at 8:45 A. M.
    " dismiss at 11:30 A. M.
    " reopen at 1:00 P. M.
    " dismiss at 4:00 P. M.

7. Visit to the Blessed Sacrament, 2 P. M. On the Missions, 5 P. M.

COMMON OBSERVANCES. 21

8. Supper, 5:30 P. M.
9. Spiritual Lecture on Missions, 8 P. M.
10. Night Prayers, 10 minutes for General Examen, Points of Meditation for the morning, 8:30 P. M.
11. Novenas are said at the Mother House at 5 P. M.,—on the Mission, at a time specified by the Superior.
12. Hour for retiring varies with the hour of rising, either 9 or 9:30 P. M., at the Mother House, but on the Missions, 9:30 P. M.

# CHAPTER III.

### SILENCE AND MODESTY,

1. The rule of silence being one of those fundamental laws on which the perfection of the religious life greatly depends, its practice is of the utmost importance to us, and hence our Rev. Founders have made it of obligation among us, in the hours specified in our Rules for its observance.

2. The chief object for this strict silence is to enable us to preserve the recollection and sense of the Presence of God, so necessary to maintain us in the spirit of our vocation amid the numerous distractions incident to our manner of life as Christian Teachers, and to enable us worthily to unite our duties and actions to those of our blessed models, Jesus, Mary and Joseph, in their holy life at Nazareth.

As exterior silence is of little value when not accompanied by interior recollection, we must endeavor to unite both in our conduct, by keeping a strict guard over the senses, particularly the eyes, lest our mind, amid this exterior silence, be more disturbed by vain and frivolous thoughts than if surrounded by worldly tumult. The spirit of silence ought so to penetrate the whole character of a Religious, as to subdue and correct whatever tendency there may be in her to a noisy, bustling manner of acting, whether in the Community, or in her intercourse with seculars. *Interior recollection is the *silence* or *solitude* of the *soul*. Without the *practice* of this *interior silence*, exterior silence is of little avail.

3. Our strictest or "solemn silence" lasts from night prayers till after morning Meditation, that the mind may be wholly occupied with the preparation for that most important duty. In proportion as we are more or less faithful to this custom, will be the facility with which we shall meditate.

4. To maintain this spirit of recollection in all our duties, we have always been required to observe silence and keep the eyes modestly cast down, not only in the streets and churches, but in the different apartments of our house, particularly in the *dormitories, refectories, halls* and *wardrobes;* in these places we must keep silence at *all* times, unless necessity or charity requires us to speak.

5. And as the silence may be broken by un-

necessary noise, as well as by loud conversation, we should avoid precipitation in walking and other actions, cultivate a gentle manner of handling furniture, dishes, etc., by which noise might be caused; also of opening and closing doors and walking through the house, particularly during the night.

6. We must guard against the curious desire to see and hear all that happens; and in the missions especially, must we refrain from approaching doors or windows, and much more, from going into the streets to look at processions or shows of any kind. If a pious lady in the world would not be guilty of such imprudence, how much more guarded should a Religious be.

7. The manner of passing through the Convent should be indicative of religious tranquillity, modesty, self-possession and recollection. In short, always, and on all occasions, it should be suited to the time, place and occupation, and in harmony with our holy profession.

8. While walking through the streets we should guard against unnecessary conversation, preserve a strict watchfulness over our whole conduct, and keep an even pace. Also in traveling, we must avoid loud or useless talking, or anything that might attract the attention of strangers.

9. The rule, which says, Local Superiors cannot grant leave to a Sister to remain away from her mission over night, does not apply to our mission houses in the same city; yet these visits should be restricted to necessity and charity.

10. In visits that we may be obliged to make to the other houses of the Congregation, the rule of silence must not be violated without necessity, through a mistaken idea of courtesy. The Sisters are always allowed to give one another a most affectionate greeting, but, unless permission be obtained, no further conversation should be held. Even in recreation time, the Sisters must guard against speaking of matters which belong exclusively to Superiors.

11. In speaking to gentlemen, Sisters should preserve a grave and earnest deportment, and guard against all levity.

Each Mission house must be provided with a gong or call-bell, in order to prevent loss of time in calling the Sisters when needed; it will also preserve order and prevent the violation of silence.

12. The conversation of Sisters with visitors should, as much as possible, be on edifying, or at least useful, subjects; and they should never allow visitors to indulge in topics opposed to charity, but should endeavor to lead such conversations

into a better channel, and never neglect an opportunity for a pious word or remark.

13. In our intercourse with the pupils, Sisters should never permit the young girls of the school to make extravagant demonstrations of affection to them, or allow such familiarities as are unbecoming, such as clasping their arms around the Sisters; also silly flattery in the form of complimentary remarks for talent or personal appearance and such things. This conduct should be discountenanced at all times by the Sisters, and the pupils should be taught the impropriety of acting so, not only because it is displeasing to the Sisters, but also from a sense of the modesty and reserve of which a Catholic girl should be a model.

### RECREATION.

1. In order to sanctify our recreation, we must take it in a manner pleasing to God. To this end it must be taken in the place and at the time appointed by Obedience. For professed Sisters, the place is the Community room; for Novices, the Novitiate, and no Sister should absent herself from the common recreation, without the Superior's permission, as we all need this short relaxation, and receive benefit from this interchange of kind words and innocent gayeties.

2. As our recreation consists in pleasant con-

versation, we must endeavor to render it general and, by our amiable sweetness and sociability, contribute to the enjoyment of each and all, like the members of one family, having but one interest in view, and hoping for an eternal reunion in heaven. Hence we should avoid sadness, dejection, coldness, or indifference of countenance, words or manner, or anything that could intimate that we dislike the Community recreation or take no interest in it, boisterousness or levity, worldly conversation, introducing or continuing subjects that we perceive are disagreeable to others, unkind or ungracious remarks of anyone, mimicking or sarcasm, egotism or family affairs.

We should also abstain from interrupting others, from contradicting or contesting, from discussing the affairs and government of the Community, the individual qualifications of Sisters; in short, from all that we would object to Superiors or the other Sisters hearing.

3. During the evening recreation, the Superior may allow a part of the time to be spent in the reading aloud of a pleasant and interesting book, innocent games and amusements are not forbidden, but this kind of recreation must be exclusively among themselves.

4. To the true Religious, the time of recreation may be of great value, as in it she will find many

opportunities of practicing charity, patience, humility, and even self-denial, in a heroic degree, and gain more merit before God than by all the other duties of the day.

5. In conformity with the custom of the Mother House, recreation shall not be taken during meals in the missions.

As the duties of mission life prevent many of our Sisters from taking recreation at the times specified in our Rule, they shall be allowed, by dispensation of the Mother-General, to recreate in community room on Saturday and Sunday afternoons until 5 o'clock.

6. Recreation must not begin until the signal is given; it may be a tap of the bell or gong, and should be given immediately after the short visit to the Blessed Sacrament or oratory, so that the time be announced publicly.

### CHARITY AND POLITENESS.

1. Sisters should always treat one another with the respect and affection of true sisters, and daughters of the same Mother, the Blessed Virgin. This affection should be manifested to all, irrespective of office or position, age or nationality, as we are all dignified by our vocation to serve the Great King and Queen of Heaven, in whose sight the last and least among us may be the highest, and hold the most honorable place.

2. The young members especially should show great charity toward the more aged. A young Sister should not, for instance, take a seat while an older one is standing, nor should any Sister, while a Superior stands; and this difference must be shown in all places as common politeness demands; however, conventional rules cannot be the guide of the true Sister,—our politeness must be produced by a better motive, true kindness of heart, and sanctified by charity, "which is the bond of perfection."

3. When meeting each other at *any time*, even during silence hours, we should, while repeating the customary religious salutation, "Praise be to Jesus, Mary and Joseph," manifest our respect exteriorly, by a graceful inclination of the head.

4. If a Sister speaks to another sharply or rudely, she renders herself guilty of a violation of charity. Not only should the Sisters abstain from all impolite and unkind expressions, but they should also be careful to season their *tone* and *manner* with *sweetness* and *charity*.

5. When a Sister from another house of our Order visits us, we should treat her with all the affection and charity that we must ever manifest for one another; yet we must guard against unnecessary inquiries into the business of the other

houses, as this inquisitiveness is often a source of trouble. We must be content to know that our Superiors attend to the welfare of all, and give ourselves no concern for what belongs to others.

6. In visiting one of our houses, we first see the Superior, acquaint her with the object of our visit, and if the Blessed Sacrament be preserved in that house, go immediately to adore Our Lord and thank Him for His merciful protection, and implore His blessing on all our undertakings; we should make another visit before taking our departure.

7. In traveling, we must be attentive to one another, especially if any be in poor health, and endeavor to save them, as much as possible, all anxiety and inconvenience. We should never leave our Sisters alone, or under the care of strangers while traveling, and above all we must be careful to evince in our exterior the charity to one another that the world expects to see among us; otherwise, we may cause much disedification when we might do much good.

8. Should Sisters of another Order stop with us, we must receive them with great charity and entertain them kindly, if we have rooms for to their proper accommodation, but we are not to admit them into our refectory or Community room, during meals or recreation, nor any of our

Community exercises; and no Sister should converse with them unless by the Superior's appointment.

9. We are not allowed to make visits to Convents not of our Congregation, through ceremony. If through necessity or charity we are led to visit them, we must avoid curiously inquiring into the affairs of their Order and communicating to them matters belonging exclusively to our own. Such intercourse might be productive of much trouble, and should be avoided.

10. In our written correspondence especially with one another, we ought to bear in mind the advice of St. Francis Xavier to the members of the Society who were under his charge in India: "The letters you write to one another should be exceedingly kind and affectionate. Be particularly careful not to let a word escape your pen that might grieve or discourage them." We should meet, as it were, in our correspondence, for the same reason that we hold actual intercourse; that is, as members of the same religious family, out of pure and affectionate regard for one another, to help or seek for help in the discharge of our duties, to console in trials, to gladden by the recital of some good that God has been pleased to perform through us, etc.

Such letters will be the links of a golden chain of sweet charity, binding together the members, and even the missions of the Congregation, when distance shall have separated us, perhaps, for life. St. Francis de Sales and St. Alphonsus Liguori were particularly desirous that their spiritual children should hold this happy intercourse among themselves.

11. As expressed in our Rule, the correspondence between the Sisters and the Mother-General must be, in all cases, exempt from the supervision of the Local Superiors.

12. Postulants are permitted to write to parents and relatives *only once a month*—Novices, *once in three months*, unless in cases of necessity.

13. Politeness requires that, before entering the apartment of the Superior, or even a schoolroom in which a Sister is teaching, also offices and reception-rooms, we give notice by gently knocking at the doors. And in the schools we must teach the children to do so.

14. OF INTERFERING.—Though we should always be ready to assist one another in our separate duties, when necessary, and not wait to be asked when we see help needed, still we must guard against interfering with one another's occupation, by making suggestions or giving com-

mands that belong only to Superiors; such interference is generally prejudicial to order and charity.

15. MURMURING.—The murmuring to which this article refers is complaining of the directions, arrangements, etc., of Superiors. Few things are more calculated to hinder individual perfection, to destroy religious discipline, to disturb the peace and harmony of a Community, and to afflict Superiors, than murmuring; therefore, all should concur in carefully excluding such an evil, which, of itself, is sufficient to ruin a Community. Our Sisters should carefully abstain from either publicly or privately criticising or complaining, or in any manner manifesting to each other disapproval of the government of the house, the conduct or manner of those in authority, the reprehensions, corrections, penances, etc.

### OBEDIENCE.

1. We must never forget that our Superior holds, in our regard, the place of God, and that, having devoted ourselves entirely to the Divine service, we should look upon every Superior as an angel sent by God to direct us in the fulfillment of His holy will, and resign ourselves to her guidance, as little children in the hands of their parents.

2. We should not only honor and respect our Superiors, but manifest a true and sincere affection for them, seek and follow their opinion in the fulfillment of our duties, general and particular, and receive their advice and counsel as coming from the lips of our Heavenly Mother herself. This respect is to be shown, not only to the Mother-General and to the Local Superior, under whose charge we are placed, but to all Officers and Sisters in charge, as far as their jurisdiction extends.

3. When the Mother-General enters a room where the Sisters are assembled, they should rise to salute her, and evince, in their looks and manner, the love and reverence for her that should be in their hearts. However, the best evidence of love that we can give our Superior is to lighten, as much as is in our power, her most painful burden, by our willingness to comply with her every wish, and the strict observance of our Rules.

### HOLY POVERTY.

1. Our Sisters should remember that the property of the Community belongs to those who have made themselves poor for the love of our Lord, and that He will not permit the goods of His servants to be destroyed or wasted with impunity. Therefore, we must be very careful of

everything in our charge—such as clothing, books, or whatever is given us for our personal use or the needs of our several duties, as loving children defend from injury all that belongs to their parents.

2. As no Sister may have or dispose of anything as her own, we procure what we call the "Small Permissions," which includes permission to make use of such articles of furniture as we need for the performance of our duties; to lend and borrow thimbles, scissors, thread, pins, needles, handkerchiefs and articles of headdress. But we must remember that the "Small Permissions" do not extend to presents, however trifling; for these we must have special permission.

At the Mother House these "permissions" are asked on the third Friday of each month; on the missions, the Local Superiors must appoint a definite time for granting them, that may be convenient at that place. Such permissions should be renewed once a month.

3. No Sister should appropriate to her own use an article destined for another, or used by another, without the knowledge of the latter, and the permission of the Superior for the transfer. Nor are we permitted to open desks, drawers or trunks belonging to another Sister, without her

knowledge and permission; but, to Superiors, all such things are free and open.

4. When presents are given to a Sister, she should bring them immediately to the Superior, mention from whom she received them, and leave them at her disposal. Superiors shall not permit the Sisters to retain such presents as are either superfluous or valuable; neither shall they allow them to retain books, periodicals, etc., presented to them from any source. Each Sister is allowed a Prayer Book, Rule Book, Office Book, and an "Imitation of Christ." It is the duty of each Superior to supply all necessary reading matter for the Sisters intrusted to her care.

5. That we may not waste the time spent in recreation, each Sister is required to provide herself with some light work during that time. If she has no work suitable, she can apply to the Superior for it, that even that short period may for the Sisters not pass uselessly.

6. Sisters who receive school funds from the pupils, or revenues from any source, must be scrupulously exact in delivering them to the Superior, and never appropriate the smallest sum to any purpose without her knowledge and permission. And Superiors must remember that their position gives them no right to incur, or allow, useless expenditure—either for the house or for individuals.

7. To prevent abuse of clothing, the Sisters on the Missions may wear old black house veils, while cleaning their school-rooms or other departments. They should also have for the same purpose a black calico or old serge habit.

8. No Sister should be guilty of using perfumes or any such worldly vanities.

9. The primitive spirit of our Congregation is one of humility and simplicity, and opposed to all extravagance or unnecessary expense in our manner of living; should a mission house not be self-supporting, we are not allowed to contract debt, but apply to the Mother-General for aid or advice.

10. Should persons apply to us for help in their need, the Superior of the house may give them food, clothing, or whatever they most need, seldom money—but always mindful of her Vow of Poverty, and with the general or special permission of the Mother-General.

11. It is customary for each of the missions to contribute toward the support of the Novitiate according to its means.

12. The furniture of our houses should be in keeping with the poverty we profess.

*Parlor.*—In our parlors, only cane-seated chairs, ingrain carpet, plain tables, etc., are allowed. No upholstered chairs or sofas, Brussels carpet, marble-topped tables, lace curtains, lambrequins, or valuable gold frames, are admissible, except in our boarding-schools; and even there, these articles must not be elaborate.

*Community - Room.*—Our Community-rooms are furnished with long tables, chairs with cane or wooden seats, cheaply-framed pictures. The floors may be oiled, plain, or covered with cheap carpet.

*Stairs and Corridors.*—The stairs and corridors may be oiled, or stained and polished, or covered with cheap carpet, matting, or oilcloth.

*Refectory.*—Our Refectories are furnished with long tables, in which are drawers containing knife, fork and spoon, for the use of each Sister. These tables are covered with oilcloth. Glassware, chinaware and silver-plate are inadmissible, except for the use of visitors.

Wooden chairs are used for seats, and a few cheap pictures in plain frames, a reading desk and crucifix complete the furniture of the Refectory.

*Chapel.*—Our Chapels may be as richly ornamented as the circumstances of our houses will permit.

*Food.*—The food, though simply served, ought to be such in quantity and quality as is calculated to nourish the Sisters, and enable them to discharge our holy duties vigorously. Great care should be taken that the food be well cooked, and served hot and comfortably. Though the Sisters not only may, but ought to be glad to have an opportunity afforded them of practicing mortification and poverty, in receiving badly-dressed, uncomfortable food, or having to wait for it, those who prepare or serve it so fail sadly in their duty to God, the Community and their own perfection.

A light lunch, which must always be taken in the refectory, is allowed to those whose laborious duties or delicate state of health seem to require it.

*Avoiding Waste.*—In a spirit of poverty, the Sisters should take care not to waste food, by leaving fragments of anything in such a state as would be unfit to be presented to the Community again.

*Clothing.*—Each Sister is allowed for her use the following articles:

2 full suits of serge.
1 serge cloak.
1 black woolen shawl.
1 black merino shawl.
2 pairs of plain leather shoes—front-laced.
1 pair of plain leather slippers, if necessary.
1 pair of overshoes.
1 pair of rubbers.

12 handkerchiefs.
2 flannel skirts.
1 winter underskirt.
1 summer underskirt.
3 calico night-dresses.
3 plain night-caps.
4 suits summer underwear.
4 pairs of summer hose.
3 pairs of winter hose.
3 full suits winter underwear.
4 towels. Corsets if necessary.

4 pieces of each article of the headdress, except veils, of which two black ones are needed, and three hoods.

Besides the above, Superiors will see that each Sister engaged in manual labor be supplied with—

2 old serge or black calico habits.
4 calico aprons.
2 old serge or black calico capes.

When Sisters are changed from one house to another, the Superior of the house they leave must carefully examine their trunks, and renew what is necessary of the above-named articles.

# CHAPTER IV.

### PENANCES.

As in all well-ordered Governments discipline is maintained by Law, and its infractions punished according to the gravity of the offense, so in religious Communities where the Rule is the Law, and the members bind themselves to its observance, it becomes necessary, knowing how prone nature is to relaxation, to defend and maintain strict observance of Rule, by submission to penance as a reparation for faults committed, and as defense against temptation. Father Rodriguez says, "The law is then in as great force and vigorous observance as if it had been but newly made when care is taken to punish him who breaks it; so in a religious order when there is no fault committed against the Rule that is not presently followed by a penance, we may then say that observance of rule is in its vigor; but when on the other hand there are frequent violations and no punishments, it is true to say that the Rules are no longer observed, and a little later, that the Rules no longer have any force, and that the contrary usage has abolished them." Book 1, Ch. 18.

In this spirit, and also to prevent abuses that might arise from the indiscriminate use of penances, we append a few acts of penance in use among us and approved by our holy founders; and Local Superiors must be very cautious in inflicting them, lest when they seek to heal they only wound. And in extreme cases, they should consult the Mother-General before imposing the penance appointed for any serious fault.

1. To absent oneself from the public visit to the Blessed Sacrament, from the recitation of the Office of the Blessed Virgin, from the half-hour's spiritual lecture or any other common Spiritual Exercise, without sufficient cause and permission from the Superior, should be acknowledged in the chapter of faults in the presence of the Community, and receive such a penance as may prevent the recurrence of such acts of negligence. It should be some extra devotional exercise.

2. Uncharitable remarks made of a Sister should be partially repaired by asking pardon of all in whose presence such remarks were made, on account of the scandal given.

This reparation should be made, at the latest, before retiring.

3. Unnecessary noise, caused by slamming doors, walking heavily through the house, particularly at night, handling dishes or furniture roughly, etc.; all such things are opposed to the spirit of religious silence, and should have an appropriate penance, such as an immediate acknowledgment to the Superior, or the recitation of the "De Profundis" or the Pater or Ave for a stated intention, at a convenient time.

4. An obstinate unwillingness to obey when required to do a certain duty, not above her strength or capacity, subjects a Sister to privation of all other duties, until the required duty be fulfilled.

5. Wasteful extravagance in the care or use of food, clothing, fuel, etc., should have an appropriate penance, as such faults are serious infringements of the Vow of Poverty.

By her punctuality in acknowledging her faults against the Rule, a Sister shows an earnest desire of overcoming them, and of living in a manner worthy of God's service; and as our manner of life is exempt from extraordinary fasts or penitential austerities, she will rejoice to accept and fulfill these little "Penances" in a right spirit.

6. PRIVATION OF OFFICE. — Should a Local Superior be so void of principle as to violate the

regulation of the Rule which restricts her in regard to letters written to the Mother-General by the Sisters, or by the Mother-General to the Sisters, she proves herself unworthy of her office, and should be deprived of it. Also for treating her Sisters, or even one Sister, with unkindness, so as to cause general dissatisfaction in the house, or injury to the health of a Sister, such a person is unfit to hold the position of Superior and should be relieved of her charge.

# CHAPTER V.

REGARDING THE REV. CLERGY.

"*Let the priests,*" says St. Paul, "*be esteemed worthy of double honor.*"

In the performance of our most important duty as Christian Teachers, we are required to act in concert with the Pastors of the Church, to whom our Divine Lord has committed the care of His flock; therefore, while we are honored by participation in their great apostolate, we must never forget the submission and reverence due to them; and as our venerable Founder inculcated, "We must entertain for them, at all times, the same respect and veneration as while they are at the Sacred Altar," and contribute what assistance is in our power, by instructing the children to the best of our ability, and with great fervor and zeal, especially in the Christian Doctrine.

In all our intercourse with the Rev. Clergy, we must keep in mind that they are the representatives and ministers of Jesus Christ upon earth, and, in our conversations with them, be ever mindful of the respect due their sacred character.

We must impress the same sentiments on the minds of the children, and guard them against the dangerous, but too prevalent, custom of criticising the words and action of priests, in a spirit of censure or disrespect, remembering the words of the Holy Ghost, *"Touch not the Lord's Anointed."*

When we are sent to take charge of a school, we must first pay our respects to the Rev. Pastor, ask his blessing and advice concerning any arrangements that it may be necessary to make with the Congregation relative to the school, and always defer to his judgment and experience in all matters relating to the religious instruction of the children.

When Clergymen visit our schools, we should ask them to bless the children, the latter having been instructed to receive the blessing of a priest with the same faith and reverence as if our Lord Himself were come to bless them.

In regard to the custom of the children's making a present to their Rev. Pastor at Christmas, or some other special occasion, consideration must be had for the means of the pupils. All cannot be expected to contribute alike, but only as each can reasonably afford.

Besides, they must all understand the real nature and object of such gifts—that they are a token of gratitude, expressive of the children's affection and respect for him, and of their congratulations, on the occasion of his feast day, etc. Through the instrumentality of their respective teachers, the Superior will ascertain the wish of the pupils as to what the gift is to be, and she will gratify their wishes as far as may be appropriate.

# CHAPTER VI.

### INTERCOURSE WITH SECULARS.

1. The intercourse of the Sisters with seculars may be productive of good or evil to the former, and should be limited to the strictest necessity; therefore our Rules require that we have a companion with us in the transaction of business with externs, both within and without our own houses—that we be to one another visible guardian Angels, and witnesses of our conduct and words.

2. In entertaining visitors Sisters should avoid all vanity or affectation, preserve a quiet and natural demeanor, guard equally against levity and affected piety, speak on religious subjects when desirable, but never in a dogmatic tone or manner; be simple and affectionate toward their relatives, and guard against curious inquiries about people and matters that do not concern them. When there is need of continuing the visit, after the half-hour prescribed, they must seek permission from the Superior. After leaving

the parlor they should, if possible, pay a visit to the Blessed Sacrament.

3. When a Sister perceives visitors on the grounds, or in the corridors, she should avoid meeting them, if she can do so without attracting notice; should it not be possible to avoid them gracefully, let her salute politely in passing, without looking to recognize them. If any of the party happens to be an acquaintance, and salutes her as such, she courteously returns the salutation and passes on unless directed to remain. The Sisters should carefully avoid looking around when visitors enter the room in which they are. The necessity of acting on all occasions with politeness and self-possession can not be too much urged.

4. It is customary for our Sisters to visit the sick, especially the poor, when time permits; but we are not allowed to attend funerals of seculars, not even relatives.

5. In these visits we are not permitted to take any refreshment, except a drink of lemonade or water, and never take a meal unless compelled by necessity, such as distance from home.

6. We are not permitted to attend evening services in public churches, without special permission from Mother-General; and Superiors should see that our houses are closed to all who

are not members of the Community at 8 P. M. Priests and physicians in the discharge of their duties excepted.

7. This rule does not apply to traveling.

8. By dispensation of the Mother-General we are permitted to attend first Mass on Christmas morning.

# CHAPTER VII.

## MISCELLANEOUS CUSTOMS.

1. LOCAL SUPERIOR.—The Local Superior must fully understand that every moment of her time should be given to the superintendence of the house and school over which she is placed. Besides, when the school is not too large, she may, as far as possible, perform the duty of the Sister Directress or delegate a part of this duty to the principal teacher. By having fixed hours for her several duties, and adhering, as far as possible to this regulation, she may easily fulfill them, and thus avoid unnecessary correspondence with persons, either within or without the Community, and long and untimely conversations with externs, by which time is wasted. By observing these regulations she may save herself and her Sisters serious annoyance.

2. SISTER DIRECTRESS.—In our academies and other schools, where a separate "Sister Directress" is not needed, the Local Superior may assume the duty of Directress, or delegate to the

principal teacher as much of it as she thinks proper.

3. THE INFIRMARY.—While in the Infirmary, and under the physician's care, a Sister cannot be visited by her relatives or friends until she is convalescent, and then she can receive them in the parlor or reception-room. In case of chronic illness the members of her family may be permitted to see her in the infirmary about once in three months, and then only one or two at a time, and for half an hour. In case of danger of death the parents of a Sister may, by dispensation from the Mother-General, be admitted to see her for a short time, according to circumstances.

4. ENTRANCE OF POSTULANTS.—In order to preserve regularity, Postulants are admitted into our Novitiate only on four days in the year, viz.: On the feast of the Help of Christians, May 24th, on the feast of the Nativity B. V. M., Sept. 8th, on the feast of St. Joseph, March 19th, and on the feast of the Immaculate Conception, Dec. 8th.

5. VISITS TO THE MOTHER-GENERAL.—When a Local Superior finds it necessary to consult the Mother-General verbally rather than by letter, she must first write for permission to go to her; before leaving her Mission she should appoint a Sister to attend to her duty until her return. At the Mother House, Local Superiors shall take the

COMMON OBSERVANCES. 53

places allotted them by the order of profession.

6. VISITATIONS.—The Sister Visitor should notify the Superior of the house to be visited at least one week before her arrival, in order that she may prepare her accounts. In the visitation of the schools the Sister Visitor should spend one day in each schoolroom of the Mission visited in order to become fully acquainted with the method and order of the school, and the progress of the pupils. The Visitation should open with the prayer, "Come Holy Ghost," etc., and close with the "Magnificat." The Sister Visitor has no jurisdiction outside of her visitation.

7. LETTERS TO MOTHER-GENERAL.—Every Sister should write to the Mother-General twice in a year, and as often besides as she may find necessary. Each Sister must write to the Mother-General for permission to make her vows anew when her time has expired for which she took them. Reports of receipts and expenses of the Mission houses are to be sent to the Mother-General quarterly, in as condensed a form as possible.

8. TERM OF NOVITIATE.—After the three months' probation, Postulants, if considered suitable candidates for our Community, shall make a Spiritual Retreat of three days previous

to their reception. Having passed two years from the time of taking the religious habit in the Novitiate, and having proved themselves worthy in every way, they may be admitted to Profession, in accordance with Art. 4, Sec. 15, of our Constitution.

9. "St. Joseph's Day."— St. Joseph being our special Patron, we celebrate his feast March 19th as a holy day of obligation throughout the entire Order. The Local Superior of each Mission will obtain from the Rev. Pastor a dispensation from school duties that the Sisters may have time to attend the spiritual exercises prescribed, viz.: The office as on Sundays, an extra hour of Adoration, and, when possible. Benediction of the Blessed Sacrament.

10. Feast of St. James.—As a tribute of love and gratitude to the memory of our Saintly Founder, we propose to observe the feast of St. James, July 25th. as a day of great devotion, and to Communicate for the repose of his soul.

11. Novenas.—Suitable Novenas are to be made, in preparation for the feasts of Christmas, Circumcision of our Lord, the Purification, Visitation, Nativity, Assumption, Immaculate Conception and Annunciation of the Blessed Virgin, the feast of Help of Christians and All Saints, also of St. Joseph and St. Patrick. The sacristan

will remind the Superior of the approach of each feast, that she may appoint the Novena to be said; and the special devotions for the months of March, May, June, October and November are to be faithfully performed in the Mission Houses as well as at the Mother House.

12. OF READING.—Superiors must carefully guard against the indiscriminate use of books, for either public or private reading, in the Community, and discard whatever might have an evil tendency. In conformity with our holy Rule, none but "spiritual reading" shall be introduced at meals. Suitable books for table reading are the works of Mueller, Faber, Ullathorne, Lives of the Saints, History of the Church, etc. During supper we should read a chapter of the New Testament, and if any time remains, read the life of a Saint.

13. MASSES FOR THE DEAD.—The Masses for the Dead to which our Rule refers are one for the repose of the souls of our Very Rev. Founder and the deceased Sisters, and one for the souls of all the faithful departed, and are to be procured each month at the Mother House. In the missions a Mass for each Sister deceased is to be said as soon as possible after her death.

14. When the Local Superior perceives that a Sister's health is so impaired that she is not

able to fulfill her duty, both she and the Sister should write to the Mother-General and inform her of the matter, and she shall decide whether the Sister is to remain at the Mission or return to the Mother House.

15. In our Missions the Sisters engaged in household duties will carefully avoid all intercourse with the pupils. When addressed by the children concerning any matter let them refer them gently and politely to the Sisters who have charge of the schools.

16. Music teachers must so order their time that all the pupils in their respective classes will receive the full time allotted to each one's lesson and practice.

17. Let the Sisters guard against allowing the children to remain longer than the proper time, either in school or music rooms, after their lessons or dismissal. Such waste of time is productive of much disorder. The Sisters should remember that in devoting themselves to God they have consecrated every moment of their future lives to be faithfully employed in His service, therefore they should not suppose that what time remains between one duty and another is at their disposal. No, for all belongs to God; and we must be most careful not to let the least portion of time pass unprofitably. Hence great purity of intention is

necessary, as well as diligence and application. All that time is misspent which is not referred to God in the accomplishment of His holy will.

18. It is the duty of the Sister Directress or her representative, in each Mission, to see that the schools are opened and dismissed in an orderly manner, and that the pupils do not loiter about the school grounds after hours.

19. Before opening a new Mission, the Mother-General or Sister Visitor should visit the place, see that the Sisters' dwelling and school are properly furnished, and make all necessary arrangements with the Rev. Pastor for the support of the school and the Sisters.

20. The Sisters shall never have their photographs taken without permission from the Mother-General. Nor shall they write in autograph albums without the same permission.

21. In case extra recreation be given in the evening it is the duty of the Superior to see that it does not extend beyond 8:30 P. M. without great necessity.

22. Sisters are not to accompany Postulants to the Mother House without special permission of the Mother-General.

23. The Sisters do not write or receive letters in Lent or Advent except on business.

# CHAPTER VIII.

### RELIGIOUS DRESS.

1. Though uniformity be desirable in everything among us, it is particularly so in regard to our dress, which should be always neat as becomes Religious, and of such material as our duties require. The dress now in use in our Community is the same that was approved by our venerated Founder, Rev. Father Donaghoe, and blessed by Rt. Rev. Bishop Loras, and our Superiors must not allow any part of this dress to be changed, without the express wish of the whole Congregation.

The material to be used in our dress is designated in our Rule. The cloak should be lined with thin black flannel, and must be worn by all in Winter; the shawl to be worn in Summer is shawl merino.

2. The street dress must be worn in public churches during Divine Service on Sundays. It should be always worn in the street, in visiting the sick, in shopping, etc., also in street cars and

omnibuses. When traveling on ships or steamboats, we are allowed to wear our house dress.

3. No Sister should appear in the chapel or oratory except in full religious dress, through respect for Our Lord's presence, no more than she would appear in the parlor, before a person of rank or dignity.

4. Our street dress is a cloak or shawl according to the season, a bonnet made of black cambric and a veil of black barege, which should be worn over the face while on the street. Black gloves or mittens may be worn in Winter, and in Summer if considered necessary; but never gloves of an expensive kind.

5. In order to preserve uniformity in the make of our habits, we subjoin a list of the depth of hems and length of veils to be worn by the Sisters, both for house and street dress:

Hem of habit sleeve when finished $\_\_2$ inches.
" " apron " " $\_\_\tfrac{1}{2}$ inch.
" " veil (house) " " $\_\_\tfrac{1}{2}$ "
" " collar, " " $\_\_\tfrac{3}{4}$ "
" " cap border, " " $\_\_1\tfrac{1}{8}$ inches.
" " veil (street) " " $\_\_1$ inch.

Length of house veil for a tall Sister,
(finished) $\_\_66$ inches.
" " " medium sized, " $\_\_64$ "
" " " small sized, " $\_\_60$ "

Length of street veil for a tall Sister,

(finished) --40 inches.
" " " medium sized, " --38 "
" " " small sized, " --36 "

Let the Superior appoint a Sister in each Mission to inspect the clothing in general, that this uniformity be preserved in material and make.

6. While in the Novitiate, the young Sisters must learn to prepare and arrange their head-dress, that they be not dependent on one another afterward for it. It would be well to do this during recreation, so as not to occupy therein the time of more important duties.

7. Sisters must be careful to have their clothing properly marked, so as to avoid unnecessary trouble in the laundry.

8. White stockings and low shoes or slippers are not to be worn in the streets.

9. The Superiors should watch over the observance of these customs, and carefully exclude innovations; for on this depends uniformity, which is so essential to the best interests of the whole Congregation. *Let them remember that only necessary dispensations can be allowed.* These customs should be read aloud for the Community in Ember Week.

# CHAPTER IX.

### REGARDING SCHOOLS.

1. It is from the motives that animate us, that all our actions are pleasing or displeasing to God. As Religious, and especially as Religious *Teachers*, how much more does this apply to us than those trying to sanctify themselves in the world.

2. The end of our Institute being the salvation of our souls, worked out in the salvation of our neighbor through the education of youth, how deeply penetrated we should be with the importance of fitting ourselves thoroughly for this sublime vocation. Of one thing, then, let us be convinced from the beginning, that we can never attach our pupils to us and cause them to take a pleasure in acquiring a knowledge of our Holy Religion, unless we can justly merit their confidence and that of their parents, in our ability as efficient teachers, if both one and the other find not in our schools what they could find in others. Let us, then, acquire and impart secular knowledge with a view to this, and with a holy and in-

telligent zeal, keep our schools progressive with the times in which we live; by inventiveness and forethought utilize our knowledge and our time to advance our pupils judiciously, and thus secure for our schools a good name, which will be the bait to draw young and innocent souls from the schools of infidelity and immorality.

3. The profession of teaching is so fraught with interests that are to tell both for time and eternity, that to assume such a duty without study or preparation is a responsibility that the reflective mind must instinctively shrink from with fear. And this dread responsibility cannot be avoided once we enter the profession, for by our example—by our very presence alone—we teach for good or for evil, whether we will it or not. As Religious, we have not assumed this great charge; Obedience has directed us; but individually we must labor strenuously, according to the spirit of our vocation, by prayer and study, to discharge this duty in a manner worthy of teachers through Obedience.

4. We are, to a certain degree, responsible for the bodily growth and the health of our children, either of which, and perhaps both, may be impaired by our culpable ignorance of the laws of health, and from overtaxing the mind. Parents may be as often to blame in this respect as teach-

ers, but on account of our profession, we ought to be better informed. Gymnastic or Calisthenic exercises, properly taught, will improve both the health and appearance of our pupils, and also aid in the discipline of the school.

5. For the moral training of our pupils we are no less responsible than for their physical. Home culture and other influences may often retard—maybe counteract—all our efforts to ennoble a child's nature; but let us not be discouraged by the obstacles that may arise, bearing in mind that as their bodily and intellectual faculties are strengthened by exercise, so, by our constant inculcation of truth and honesty of purpose as the groundwork of a great moral character, and this not only by word, but by example—for children are quick to learn from this—we may hope to see, if not immediately, at least in time, a corresponding development of their moral faculties.

6. And, if we are to hold ourselves responsible, and gravely so, for our pupils' physical, intellectual and moral training, what are we to feel concerning the crowning motives of all our endeavors, of all our labors—the Religious training of the thousands and thousands of precious souls committed to our charge?

7. That we may not lose sight of the end for which we have undertaken all, but more especially

this most responsible of our duties, we must daily invoke the assistance of our Blessed Mother and St. Joseph to help us in its fulfillment, and to obtain for us purity of intention, that we may see in each of our pupils the Holy Child, Jesus, and so act toward each that we may merit the blessing of this Divine Child, both for our pupils and for ourselves.

8. As to their Religious training, then, we must scrupulously instruct the children according to their age, in all the practices and duties of Religion, such as to make the Sign of the Cross correctly, to recite the Lord's Prayer, the Hail Mary, the Apostles' Creed, the Confiteor and the Acts of Contrition, Faith, Hope and Charity perfectly and devoutly. We must also teach them how to examine their conscience, and how to prepare for and make their Confession. They must be taught how to assist at Mass—uniting their intentions with those of the Priest, in offering the Holy Sacrifice for the intentions of the Church, that they may participate in Her merits. They must also be taught the practice of making mental prayer, using subjects suited to their capacity. All who have made their First Holy Communion should be taught this practice daily. Teach them that to meditate means to think; that to meditate on a religious subject is

simply to think on it as we would about the preparation of a lesson, or about some game we have planned and are going to tell our playmates—show them how, in religious thinking, or meditation as it is generally called, we first read or listen to the fact or truth placed before us—then think how we stand before God in the light this truth has thrown upon our mind. What virtue does it show us that we stand in need of, or what vice or sin do we discover in ourselves? Then as naturally as we think, comes the thought, "What must we do?" and so follows the resolution, either to strive to acquire the virtue, if wanting, by performing such or such acts, or to root out the evil, avoiding or refraining from what we know has been the cause of our yielding to temptation. By some such explanation as this, clearly, simply and earnestly given, children will understand and be impressed with the importance of meditation, and so be led to think, and above all to think rightly, for if the young mind learns to reflect upon religious truths it will soon conform its motives and actions to this mode of thinking, and so cannot fail to think and act rightly—having a correct basis of thought. This is the great want of our day, and with the Prophet we may say, "*With desolation is the land made desolate, because there is none that considereth in the heart."* Teach the children to meditate, and for them, at least, much of this desolation will be obviated. Not less important for them to be taught is how to make the daily particular and general examen, making them understand how easy a means this is to overcome their faults and to advance in virtue. Impress deeply on their minds the end for which they were created, and the absolute necessity each one is under of working out his own salvation, and therefore the constant need of prayer and the wonderful strength acquired by it against temptation; teach them, then, ejaculatory prayers, and a great devotion to their Guardian Angel, for these prayers and this devotion will help to keep them in the Presence and Grace of God.

9. Teach and explain to them the mysteries of our Holy Religion and how to meditate on them when reciting the Rosary, also how to perform the devotion of The Way of the Cross. They should be taught hymns, and required to sing them frequently, for by this means they learn many religious maxims and principles that cannot readily be effaced from the mind.

10. We must impress the minds of the children with the greatest respect and veneration for the Rev. Clergy and for the ceremonies of the Church, and we must not be intimidated in our religious

instructions to the children, by the presence of non-Catholic pupils; though we should be careful not to make any remarks that could wound the feelings of such. However, persons of other denominations know that we instruct our children in our Holy Religion, and, therefore, when non-Catholic children attend our schools they expect to hear this instruction and never expect any concession to be made on their account. They shall be required to kneel during prayers in school, and to conform generally to the external religious requirements of the school; and we must carefully watch over our Catholic children while obliged to associate with those of other denominations, that their morals be not corrupted, nor their faith undermined by infidel or Protestant influence or example.

11. Sisters should carefully avoid speaking to any pupil of the affairs of the Convent, or of another pupil's progress, disposition, or family affairs of any kind; nor tell the pupils the names, family names, of any of the Sisters, especially of those engaged in teaching them, and avoid showing any partiality to one or a few pupils in preference to the others; such conduct is anything but religious.

12. Let each Sister devote all the time allowed to her own classes, whether in thes choolroom or

on the play ground. She should avoid all unnecessary intercourse with another Sister's pupils.

13. The Sisters engaged in teaching must scrupulously employ the hour allotted for study, and also any time left after the performance of their several household duties, in the preparation of the lessons to be taught in school and in their own improvement; to accomplish this latter requirement, they must adopt some order in their method of study. Though, perhaps, much cannot be done at a time, still let them not be discouraged; a little study every day will show surprising results; if anyone fails, having the proper means, it will be from want of utilizing the time at her disposal.

14. The Sisters teaching in the Primary and Intermediate Departments must be very particular in this point, as their grades require almost constant oral teaching; the Sisters must qualify themselves to impart general elementary knowledge with ease, grammatical accuracy, and in language intelligible to the young.

15. In teaching, we must avoid two extremes, viz.: giving too much aid, or too little. When children come to us for an explanation—or even in teaching our class—we should endeavor to make them think—speak to them about the general principle which the matter under considera-

COMMON OBSERVANCES. 69

tion involves, or upon some elucidation previously given upon something similar. This should be done kindly, not in a cold or formal manner, but with a kind interest, and in a way that will set them thinking, and invite them to express their thoughts, and, crude though they be, we will often be surprised at the correctness of their reasoning. This way of teaching them, without seeming to teach, as it were, will open their minds, put them in the way of working for themselves, which is simply the only way of educating rightly, for we should remember that what is done *for* children, without due study on their part, makes but a feeble impression, and is soon forgotten.

16. We must wake up their minds by constantly calling into action their powers of observation and reasoning, and incite them to ascertain for themselves. If we do not do this, or if we do it poorly, they will grow up blind, so to speak, to the manifold beauty of God's creation; they will study none of the plans of nature that are constantly working so wonderfully above, around and beneath. But to so direct the minds of our children we ourselves must be alive to our surroundings in this beautiful world of the visible creation of God. We must acquire a general knowledge, not studying for our own gratification or pleasure simply, but as Religious, to increase

our influence and usefulness, as a means to accomplish the end of our holy vocation.

17. We must carefully study the characters of the children we teach, that we may deal with them in the way best suited to each; and if it be allowable to manifest a special interest in any one pupil, let it be in the child of inferior abilities.

18. In regard to time we must be scrupulously exact. In the morning, if we have no household duty that needs attention, repairing immediately to our schoolroom, as our Rule regarding the duties of each Sister expresses. As sometimes it may happen that a Sister is detained longer than usual, yet she must try to be in her schoolroom at least a quarter of an hour before school time.

19. We must be particular to keep our rooms neat and orderly, and require the same of the children—to keep their desks in good order—instructing them in personal neatness and polite deportment, and requiring them to put these lessons in practice while under our supervision.

20. We must watch over their conduct well during the time allotted for play; in fact, we will find, if we wish to acquit ourselves well of our responsible charge, that from the moment the children present themselves in the morning until dismissed in the evening, we will have to give

them our undivided attention. During the time of Intermission, and, of course, *never* in school, are we permitted to engage in any kind of needlework, nor in reading any book or paper, but must give our whole attention to the welfare and progress of the children while in school, and to their conduct and the care of the school furniture, etc., during the time of recreation.

21. In giving correction we will find it best to give reproof to the individual pupil in private. We will thus win the child's confidence. Every expedient must be tried before resorting to corporal punishment; still, it is a necessary form of correction; for even to know that it will be inflicted, if their conduct merit such, will often of itself preserve discipline in the school. Our Superiors deem it advisable that when obliged to administer correction in this manner we do it privately or during intermissions. We should always be calm and self-possessed in the presence of the children, but especially so when obliged to inflict corporal punishment. Make the child feel and acknowledge the gravity of his fault, and that you are pained to be forced to deal so severely with him. Girls should never be punished in this manner.

22. Animated by the spirit of our vocation, in our conduct toward each other, we should ever

evince the deepest regard and affection, especially before externs. Can they say of us as was said of the first Christians: "*Behold how they love one another!*"

23. Are we mindful of this in the presence of the children, who are daily witnesses of our reciprocal relation? What scandal if they perceive that there is not a good feeling among us; if they should see the least mark of disagreement!

24. Do not let us be deceived; children are more clear-sighted than many of us seem to suppose; a look, an impatient word, a smile even, may do more to scandalize them than years of after teaching will be able to remove.

25. To avoid such sad results let us love one another *sincerely*, "*As Christ loved us.*" By this we shall prove ourselves His disciples, and so merit His benedictions for ourselves and for our pupils.

26. Holidays are to be granted rarely. Indeed, the national holidays of the year might be considered sufficient. Still, it will help very much to attract and endear to children their own school if they are permitted to celebrate certain days of special interest to the school alone. Such, for instance, as the Patron Saints' day, the anniversary of some important event in the history of the school, etc. A little ingenuity on the part of the

teacher, judiciously carried out, will make these occasions beneficially happy ones.

27. The text books in all our schools must be Catholic, as far as possible, especially our Readers, Literatures, Geographies and Histories. But we are permitted to consult other standard authors on all subjects of interest, and to read useful, religious and educational works. According to the means of the house, the Superior may subscribe for one or two educational periodicals or papers, and for any approved religious paper or periodical of the day. When any books or papers are given to a Sister she will first submit them to the Superior.

28. As incentives to study, it is proved by experience that Monthly Reviews, followed by Reports of the same to the parents or guardians of the pupils, and semi-annual Examinations, followed by class or individual promotions, are productive of better results in the school, of better feeling among all concerned, more especially the children and their parents, than by the distribution of premiums, therefore our Sisters will adopt this method as a proper means of exciting emulation.

29. The Reviews should be held in the presence of the Rev. Pastor, Sister Superior, some of

the other Sisters, if possible, and, if expedient, a few invited friends of the pupils.

30. The Scholastic year shall be divided into two terms of five months each. At the end of each term there must be a Public Examination, to which the children's parents and the patrons and friends of the school must be invited. These Examinations must be just, thorough and complete.

31. All our words and dealings with the children tend to the formation of their character; therefore we must be particularly careful to put before them noble ends for all their actions. Teach them first to refer all their thoughts. words, and actions to God; to work for His greater honor and glory; that they owe a debt of gratitude to their parents and teachers, which they can best pay off by acquitting themselves well of their duty as pupils; their own advancement is also a commendable motive to urge them to work for, when it is not selfish in its object. Teach them to wish and to labor to be useful members of society. and that they cannot hope to be such without a good Catholic education. We should frequently examine ourselves on this. See if the principles we inculcate are of a nature to form the children to virtue, to union among themselves, to respect for their superiors, to love

for their parents. True, some will not profit by our endeavor, some will not correspond to our wishes, but our labor will not be lost on all. It will not be without some result favorable to their salvation, that the children of our schools shall have listened to so many religious instructions, shall have passed so many days in innocence and in the fear of God. Such thoughts as these must encourage us in our duty, for our Lord Himself assures us, *"He that shall do and teach, he shall be called great in the Kingdom of Heaven."*

# CONCLUSION.

"He that shall persevere to the end shall be saved."—
MATT. XXIV: 13.

"O God, Who hast called us away from the vanities of the world, and hast inflamed our hearts with a love of so exalted a vocation, Who has prepared for us a habitation in Heaven when we renounce earth, grant us the grace of perseverance, that, strengthened by the power of Thy protection, we may fulfill all the resolutions we have taken, and thus, responding to our vocation in time, we may, in eternity, possess that crown which Thou hast promised to those who persevere to the end, through Jesus Christ our Lord."

# INDEX.

|  | PAGE. |
|---|---|
| PREFACE, | 3 |

## CHAPTER I.
| | |
|---|---|
| SPIRITUAL EXERCISES, | 5 |

## CHAPTER II.
| | |
|---|---|
| GENERAL EXAMEN, | 16 |
| COMMUNITY PRAYERS, | 18 |
| CATALOGUE OF TIME, | 20 |

## CHAPTER III.
| | |
|---|---|
| SILENCE AND MODESTY, | 22 |
| RECREATION, | 26 |
| CHARITY AND POLITENESS, | 28 |
| OBEDIENCE, | 33 |
| HOLY POVERTY, | 34 |

## CHAPTER IV.
| | |
|---|---|
| PENANCES, | 41 |

## CHAPTER V.
| | |
|---|---|
| REGARDING THE REV. CLERGY, | 45 |

## CHAPTER VI.
| | |
|---|---|
| INTERCOURSE WITH SECULARS, | 48 |

## CHAPTER VII.
| | |
|---|---|
| MISCELLANEOUS CUSTOMS, | 51 |

## CHAPTER VIII.
| | |
|---|---|
| RELIGIOUS DRESS, | 58 |

## CHAPTER IX.
| | |
|---|---|
| REGARDING SCHOOLS, | 61 |
| CONCLUSION, | 76 |

www.ingramcontent.com/pod-product-compliance
Lightning Source LLC
Chambersburg PA
CBHW022142090426
42742CB00010B/1360